Heinemann InfoSearch

Crushing Avalanches

Heinemann Library
Chicago, Illinois

Louise and Richard Spilsbury

Customer Service 888-454-2279
Visit our website at www.heinemannlibrary.com

Designed by David Poole and Paul Myerscough
Illustrations by Geoff Ward
Originated by Dot Gradations Limited
Printed in Hong Kong, China by Wing King Tong

07 06 05 04 03
10 9 8 7 6 5 4 3 2 1

Library of Congress Cataloging-in-Publication Data
Spilsbury, Louise.
  Crushing avalanches / Louise and Richard Spilsbury.
      p. cm. -- (Awesome forces of nature)
Summary: Describes the causes and effects of avalanches, case studies of past avalanches, and how they can be predicted or prevented in the future.
Includes bibliographical references and index.
  ISBN 1-4034-3721-1 (lib. bdg.) -- ISBN 1-4034-4230-4 (pbk.)
  1. Avalanches--Juvenile literature. 2. Avalanches--Environmental aspects--Juvenile literature. [1. Avalanches.] I. Spilsbury, Richard, 1963- II. Title.
  QC929.A8.S65 2003
  551.57'848--dc21

                              2003001106

Acknowledgments
The author and publisher are grateful to the following for permission to reproduce copyright material:
Cover photograph by Roberta Parkin/Still Pictures.
p. 4 Still Pictures/Roberta Parkin; p. 5 AP/Lechiner; p. 7 SPL; p. 8 Venture Pix; p. 9 Yoram Porath; p. 10 South American Pictures; pp. 11, 13, 21, 26 Corbis; p. 12 Alamy; p. 14 Eric Limon Photography; p. 15 Rex Features/SIPA Press; p. 16 AP/Georg Koechler; p. 17 AP/Douglas C. Pizac; p. 18 AP/Dietner Endlicher; p. 19 AP/Rudi Blaha; p. 22 Das Fotoarchive/Marcus Matzel; p. 23 Still Pictures/Mountain Sport; p. 24 Still Pictures/Andreas Riedmiller; p. 25 Rex Features/Toby Rankin; p. 28 Still Pictures/Ask Images.

Every effort has been made to contact copyright holders of any material reproduced in this book. Any omissions will be rectified in subsequent printings if notice is given to the publisher.

Some words are shown in bold, **like this.** You can find out what they mean by looking in the glossary.

Contents

What Is an Avalanche?

When snow slides or slips down mountainsides we call it an avalanche. The word *avalanche* comes from a French word that means "descent" or fall. As the snow slides down, it smashes into ice, rocks, soil, and trees. If it hits them with enough force, they come hurtling down the mountain, too.

When do avalanches happen?

There are many avalanches every year, usually at the same times of year. They can only happen after snow has fallen and collected on mountainsides during cold seasons. Most avalanches in Europe and North America happen between January and March. Some happen later in the year, when temperatures start to rise and the snow and ice start to melt. In these conditions, big chunks of snow do not stick to the ground very well and may start to move.

An avalanche like this can come racing down a mountainside without any warning. Eyewitnesses say that a speeding mass of ice and snow like this sounds like a roaring thunderstorm.

Destructive forces

Avalanches vary in size and force. They can be slow movements of a few pounds of snow over several feet. They can also be massive shifts of hundreds of tons of snow and rock. They can speed several miles down a mountainside, like express trains.

Big avalanches can destroy anything that gets in their way. In some places, big avalanches knock down trees and affect the lives of mountain animals. In other places, they can crush whole towns and the people who live there. In these places, avalanches become terrible natural disasters.

An avalanche can bury cars, buildings, roads, animals, and people under a heavy blanket of icy snow.

AVALANCHE ⚡ FACTS

! There are perhaps a million avalanches each year around the world; most cause very little damage to people.

! Avalanches can move at up to 185 miles (300 km) per hour—that is the speed of a Formula One racing car. They usually move much faster than any person can run.

Where Do Avalanches Happen?

Avalanches happen all over the world where snow falls and there are mountains. Many of the avalanches that take place go unnoticed by people because they happen in distant, snowy places where nobody goes. Some avalanches affect people who live on or at the edge of mountain ranges. Mountain ranges where there are a lot of avalanches include the Alps in Europe, the Himalayas in Nepal and Tibet (in Asia), the Andes in South America, and the Rocky Mountains in the United States.

Avalanches often happen in exactly the same locations within these mountain areas. This is because only certain slopes are steep enough for snow to settle and to slide down.

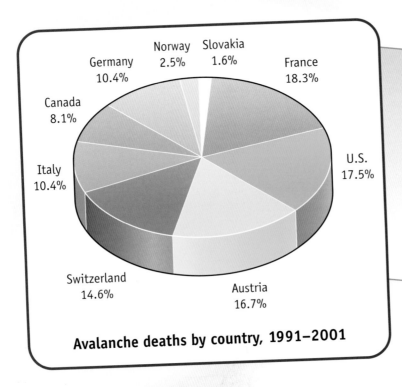

Avalanche deaths by country, 1991–2001

*Over 1,300 people died in avalanches between 1991 and 2001. This **pie chart** shows that most deaths resulting from avalanches happened in France, Austria, and the U.S.*

What Causes an Avalanche?

Snow that has already fallen and built up on a slope is called **snow cover.** Most snow cover is stable, which means it stays where it is on a slope. Some snow cover, however, is unstable, and this may start an avalanche.

Types of snow cover

Snow falls from the sky as star-shaped flakes or as rounded granules, depending on the temperature. After snow lands, it changes shape because of the weight of more snow landing on top of it and because of temperature changes. This is called settling. When flakes settle they form stable snow cover. Granules, however, roll over each other and settle as weak layers of snow. If a lot of snow falls quickly on top of a weak layer—for example in a **blizzard,** or when thick, heavy **snowdrifts** form in heavy winds—then it may form unstable snow cover. Avalanches are **triggered** by slight movements of unstable snow cover.

Snowflakes settle to form stable snow cover because their points lock together like pieces of a jigsaw puzzle.

Triggers

Sometimes small movements, such as the movement of a wild animal or the melting of a layer of snow, can **trigger** an avalanche. Some avalanches are caused by the shaking force of a loud machine or even an earthquake. However, most fatal avalanches are triggered by people.

Are all avalanches the same?

Not all avalanches are the same. There are four main types, depending on **snow cover:** dry slab, wet slab, wind, and ice.

Dry **slab avalanches** are the most common. Layers of settled snow build up to form a thick, dry snow slab which can become as brittle as a pane of glass. When triggered, it can suddenly shatter and break into big chunks of ice that slide down mountainsides at high speeds.

Wet slab avalanches happen when rain and sun weaken large slabs of snow cover. They slip down the mountainside much more slowly than shattered hard slabs. Because they are wet and heavy, they drag boulders, trees, and soil along with them.

Dry slab avalanches slip like fast sleighs over the weak snow layer underneath.

Wind avalanches are less common. Occasionally snow falls and settles as a mixture of flakes and granules, forming a loose, light powder. When an avalanche is triggered, the powder forms giant snow clouds. These snow clouds travel down slopes very quickly, creating a ferocious wind ahead of them.

AVALANCHE ⚡ FACTS

! Wind avalanches are so strong they can blast the tops off trees or the roofs off houses, a bit like a bomb.

! Anything in the path of an ice avalanche can be destroyed.

Ice avalanches are rare, but they have caused some of the worst avalanche disasters. **Glaciers** are immense slabs of ice that form on shallow slopes after years of snowfall. They usually move very slowly because they are so heavy. Sometimes huge chunks of a glacier can break off and start an ice avalanche. They may move fast, sweeping hundreds of tons of snow, rock, soil, or water in front of them.

When ice avalanches fall into water, they can cause big, destructive waves.

Yungay, Peru, 1970

Yungay is a small town in the Andes mountains, in Peru. On the afternoon of May 31, 1970, many of the town's people were listening to the soccer World Cup on the radio. At 3:23 P.M. a huge earthquake shook most of Peru. Walls and houses crumpled and whole streets split open. This destructive force was just the beginning, though—the earthquake also triggered an awesome **ice avalanche.**

Falling mountain

Mount Huascarán—the tallest mountain in Peru—is more than four miles (nearly seven km) high. It is at one end of a high-sided valley containing Yungay and several villages. Before the earthquake, a **glacier,** high on Huascarán, had been weakened as it melted during the spring. When the earthquake hit, a piece of the glacier shook loose.

> "At that time I heard a great roar coming from Huascarán. Looking up, I saw what appeared to be a cloud of dust, and it looked as though a large mass of rock and ice was breaking loose from the north peak." Mateo Casaverde, survivor

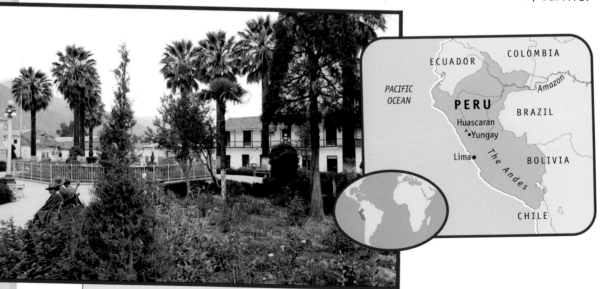

The center of Yungay in 1968. These palm trees survived the avalanche in 1970.

Speeding wave

The ice avalanche was more than half a mile (about one km) across and weighed millions of tons. It dropped nearly 2.5 miles (four km) before it hit the valley floor. It then hurtled down the valley towards Yungay, pushing an immense wave of snow, rock, soil, and water in front of it.

"The crest of the wave had a curl, like a huge breaker coming in from the ocean. I estimated the wave to be at least 80 meters [260 feet] high. I reached the high ground of the cemetery a few seconds before the debris flow struck the base of the hill." Mateo Casaverde

The wave took about three minutes to travel nine miles (fifteen km) to Yungay. The town was completely buried by the avalanche. Of the town's 25,000 inhabitants, only about 2,000 survived. It was the world's worst recorded avalanche.

This photo, taken after the avalanche, shows the valley where Yungay once stood. The town has been completely buried.

What Happens in an Avalanche?

When an avalanche happens, people do not get any warning. Sometimes people report hearing a soft "woosh" sound or a loud crack. Usually the first thing a person knows about an avalanche is being knocked over and carried down a mountainside by it.

"I heard a deep, muffled thunk as it fractured. Then it was like someone pulled the rug out from under me." Bruce Tremper, dry **slab avalanche** survivor

Tumbling

Survivors of avalanches often describe being spun around so much they do not know which way is up. They say it is a bit like being in a tumble dryer full of snow and ice. The force of moving snow is so great that people cannot control the direction they are sliding. It is difficult to slow down because avalanches speed up as they move.

This snowboarder is trying to get safely out of the way of an avalanche that is moving down the slope.

Dangers

The biggest danger in an avalanche is **suffocation.** In an avalanche, the air is so full of snow that it is hard to breathe. If people get buried under snow, usually only a tiny amount of air is trapped with them. The danger is that it will run out before rescuers reach them.

Some people are injured when the avalanche throws chunks of ice, rocks, and trees into them. Others suffer from **hypothermia**—they get so cold they become sick. Avalanches also bury buildings, cars, roads, and tunnels under tons of snow, ice, and soil.

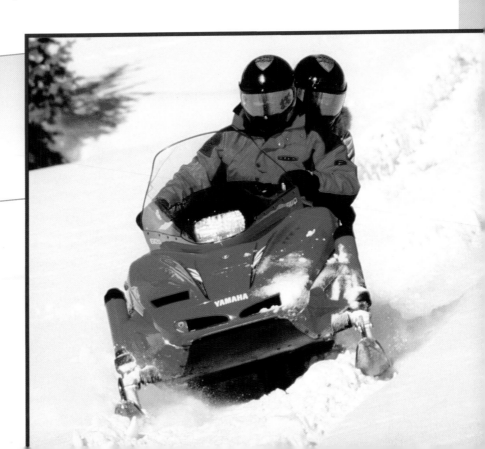

Snowmobiles are heavy and can easily trigger slab avalanches.

What should people do in an avalanche?

Here are a few things that people who get caught in an avalanche should do.

- Try to get off the moving slab of snow and ice.

- Try to grab a tree or boulder quickly before the avalanche builds up speed. This may help to slow down sliding.

- Keep moving, using the arms and legs, as if swimming hard. The greatest danger is to sink deeper into the snow.

- Try to clear a large space in front of the mouth before the avalanche stops. Then there will be a pocket of air to breathe.

- Before the snow settles, push a hand upward so that rescuers might see it. A good way of telling which way is up is to dribble some saliva (spit)—it always moves toward the ground.

When big avalanches threaten towns among snowy mountains, the people who live there need to know what to do to remain safe.

Les Orres, France, 1998

On January 23, 1998, a group of students on a school trip set off for a walk on **snowshoes** in Les Orres in the French Alps. They had several guides with them and had just spent a week learning about snow sports and snow hazards. Heavy snowfall in the area meant there was risk of avalanches, but their guides still decided to go.

> "One cannot criticize these people in such a tragic moment, but personally, I wouldn't have gone trekking today in these conditions." Gerard Bouchet, leader of one of the rescue teams

As the group walked up to a ridge above some woods, disaster struck. Their movements triggered a dry **slab avalanche** up to 985 feet (300 meters) wide, which swept them down the slope. Rescue workers later found many of the survivors stunned and clinging to trees.

Out of the party of 42 that set out, 11 people were killed and 21 were injured in the avalanche at Les Orres. Over 150 rescue workers helped rescue survivors.

Who Helps After an Avalanche?

Avalanche victims have to be found quickly because of the danger that they will **suffocate.** So, trained, expert assistance is necessary in areas where avalanches are a problem.

Getting help

Rescue teams work in particular areas of the mountains. They have detailed knowledge of avalanche **terrain**—the areas where avalanches are most likely—and how to find buried victims there. They also watch for weather changes in the mountains, and can tell when avalanches are most likely. When avalanches happen, these experts organize teams of **volunteers** to help them find survivors. They work closely with emergency services, such as the police.

> **AVALANCHE ⚡ FACTS**
>
> ! Only half of all avalanche victims survive after being trapped in snow for more than 30 minutes.

Rescue teams try to get to the avalanche area quickly, often using helicopters and snowmobiles.

Finding people

Rescuers look for avalanche clues such as broken trees and mounds of snow with debris. They also look for signs of buried people such as scattered clothing and backpacks. Buried people are usually found if rescuers can see a part of their body, such as a hand, sticking out of the snow.

Many others are found using probe lines. In a probe line, rescuers spread out in a straight line, walking slowly and quietly forward. They gently poke long, thin poles into the snow every 1.5 feet (50 cm) to find buried people.

Transceivers

If a person who is buried in the snow is wearing a **transceiver,** he or she is more likely to receive help quickly. The transceiver sends out regular signals so that rescuers, who have receivers, can pinpoint exactly where the signals are coming from. The signals lead them to the avalanche victim. Many people who live and work in avalanche areas carry transceivers.

These people have formed a probe line. If one of their poles touches something, rescuers use shovels to carefully but quickly dig the victim out.

Helping dogs

Rescuers also use working dogs to find avalanche victims. Most of the dogs are German Shepherds, but some are St. Bernards and labradors.

Rescue dogs are specially trained by their owners. First, the dogs are trained to recognize a human's smell. Then, they are trained to smell this smell through deeper and deeper snow. Most rescue dogs can find people buried up to thirteen feet (four meters), but a few have found survivors under 32 feet (ten meters) of snow. The usual reward for these dogs is playtime playing with their trainer!

Sensitive noses

People always give off a faint scent because of **bacteria** growing on their skin. Dogs can smell this scent thousands of times better than people can. If someone is caught in an avalanche, their scent spreads through the snow around them. Rescue dogs search for patches of snow where the smell is strongest.

One rescue dog with its trainer can search avalanche areas about eight times faster than twenty people in probe lines.

Medical care

Once avalanche victims have been found, many need immediate **first aid.** Rescue teams are trained to deal with injuries such as broken limbs, cuts, and bruises. They also treat **hypothermia** by gently warming the victims using special heated vests and blankets. Victims with more serious injuries are taken by helicopter to specialist hospitals where experts can treat them.

Other dangers

When avalanches hit towns or cities, large numbers of people may face other dangers. The force of an avalanche can trap people under collapsed buildings or inside cars. It can pull down **power lines** that may **electrocute** people. Powerlines can also make sparks that start fires.

Sometimes emergency services, such as the police, work with national forces, such as the army, to rescue victims. Some poorer countries have fewer rescue workers and less rescue equipment. They may ask for help from wealthier countries after a major avalanche disaster.

After an avalanche—or any other natural disaster—more victims will survive if emergency services can find them and help them quickly.

Anchorage, Alaska, 2000

The Seward Highway is the main road connecting the cities of Anchorage and Seward in Alaska. It is the route that is used for the transportation of food and other goods to people living on the Kenai peninsula. It is also one of the most avalanche-threatened roads in North America because of the high cliffs and steep slopes on either side of it.

The winter of 1999–2000 was a bad one in Alaska. Very cold weather froze the snow that had fallen. Then, temperatures rose and melted the fallen snow, making a weak layer. In January, four times the usual amount of snow fell around Anchorage. This added thousands of tons to the **snow cover** on top of the weak layer.

Warmer weather, high winds, and rainstorms **triggered** many dry **slab avalanches.** One of these avalanches flattened buildings in the city of Cordova, causing $2.6 million in damage. On February 2, 2000, several avalanches up to a half mile (one km) across covered the Seward Highway, cutting off around 2,000 people in Kenai. Tens of thousands of people had no electricity for a week after **power lines** were knocked down.

The Alaskan avalanches of 1999–2000 were a major disaster affecting thousands of people.

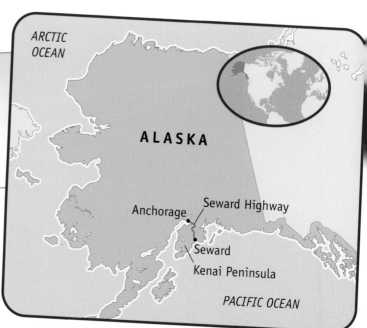

Rescue and clean-up

The National Guard, police, and other emergency services worked together to rescue stranded people quickly. Highway workers and **volunteers** cleared most of the Seward Highway using bulldozers and shovels. Helicopters dropped **explosives** to clear patches of thick snow from slopes above the road. They were cleared to prevent a big avalanche from harming the workers below. However, when three bulldozers started to clear the road of snow, strong winds above the slopes started a wind avalanche. The drivers had little warning before it hit them.

> "I could hear the windows starting to crackle and shatter. Then one popped and so did the others." Larry Bushnell, bulldozer driver

Two of the bulldozer drivers were injured slightly, but the third died. The avalanche had pushed his sixteen-ton machine 325 feet (100 meters) and it rolled upside-down. Although they faced dangerous conditions, workers eventually managed to clear the road.

Rescue and repair workers cleaning up after avalanches are often at high risk of further danger.

Can Avalanches Be Predicted?

Many people who live in and around snowy mountains make their living from **tourism.** They provide food, hotels, and lessons for winter visitors who want to ski, for example. To keep tourists safe they rely on the accurate prediction of avalanches.

Avalanche institutes

There are special avalanche **institutes** in countries such as Japan and the United States, where avalanches are a problem. Avalanche institute workers collect information about avalanche **terrain,** such as how steep mountain slopes or valleys are. They also record whether trees in wooded areas are close together or not. When trees are close together, they hold the fallen snow in place. When trees are far apart, avalanches can run between them. Avalanche institutes use all of this information to draw avalanche hazard maps. These maps show which areas are most likely to have avalanches.

RISQUE D'AVALANCHE
PROMENADE INTERDITE

NO ENTRY
RISK OF AVALANCHE

LAWINENGEFAHR
FÜR FUSSGÄNGER VERBOTEN

STRADA VIETATA PER
RISCHIO DI VALANGA

When avalanche institutes have figured out which areas are at risk of avalanches, they can warn people about the danger.

Weather and snow cover

Avalanche institutes also collect information about the weather, and especially about snowfall. They measure the amount of snow that falls each day, the direction the wind is blowing, and the air temperature. Scientists **forecast** how the weather might change and **trigger** avalanches. They use information from photographs of clouds taken by **satellites** in space and from their knowledge of **climate.**

Scientists examine **snow cover** to see if it may avalanche. By looking at the thickness and type of snow in its layers, they can see whether it has settled tightly. Snow that has not settled tightly has air spaces in it and sounds hollow when it is tapped.

Acid rain and avalanches

When **pollution** in the air mixes with rainwater, it makes acid rain. When acid rain falls on trees, it kills their leaves. If acid rain kills trees in avalanche areas, it means the trees cannot act like fences to stop or slow down avalanches.

Scientists look closely at snow cover in avalanche hazard areas by carefully digging holes called snow pits.

Can Avalanches Be Prevented?

Avalanches are natural forces. People cannot stop avalanches once they are in motion, but they can prevent thick **snow cover** from building up in the first place.

Looking after trees

Trees are an important way of making slopes stable. Trees are a natural barrier to avalanches, and their roots also help to hold **topsoil** together. When people cut down trees for **timber** or **firewood,** the topsoil is exposed and may be washed away by rain or carried away by avalanches. Eventually this may leave a surface of bare rock. Snow cover is even less stable on bare rock.

Tree protection

Even six hundred years ago people knew that trees could stop avalanches. In forested avalanche areas of Switzerland, forest inspectors punished people for damaging trees—even for picking their berries and cones. In the worst cases, the punishment was death.

People should only cut down a few trees from mountain slopes so there are enough trees left to help stop avalanches.

Breaking up snow

The best way of preventing avalanches is to remove unstable snow before it becomes a hazard. Skilled people set off small, controlled avalanches. Ski **rangers** regularly visit avalanche **terrain** after heavy snowfall. They look for overhangs of snow on ridges. They test the strength of snow cover by zigzagging across slopes on skis and jumping up and down on the snow.

Army teams use rifles and cannons to "shoot the slopes" with **explosives.** From up to a mile (two km) away they blow up suspect snow on large slopes and overhangs. Ski rangers and mountain patrol teams sometimes use avalaunchers—cannons powered by gas. Unlike guns they make no noise when they fire, which is better because loud noise can **trigger** an avalanche. People also use helicopters and planes to shoot the slopes in less accessible areas.

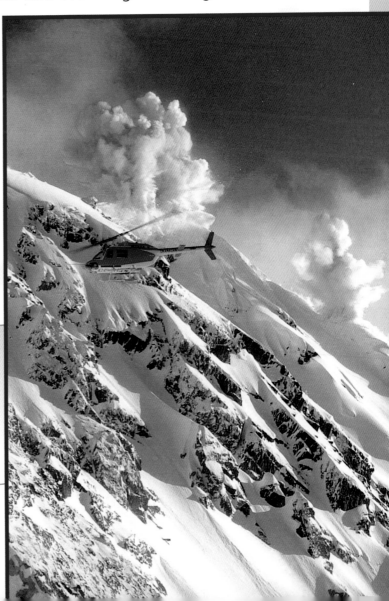

The two clouds are actually explosions, which have started a controlled avalanche on a mountain. The explosives were set off by a team traveling by helicopter.

How Do People Prepare for Avalanches?

Not all avalanches can be prevented. So, people who live and work in areas threatened by avalanches have to be prepared when disaster strikes.

Many villages and towns build avalanche breakers on the slopes above them. These are strong barriers that can change the direction in which an avalanche is moving. The barriers are sometimes big heaps of rock and soil. Or, they may be V-shaped concrete structures about 13 feet (4 meters) high and 325 feet (100 meters) long.

When people build houses on a mountain, they usually give them long sloping roofs. A sloping roof makes it more likely that avalanches will slide over them and not knock down the house.

Some roads and railway tracks are protected from smaller avalanches by special tunnels. The tunnels are called galleries. They keep people and vehicles inside from being buried in snow and rock.

These barriers will help to trap snow that falls in winter. Then it will not slip toward the buildings farther down the valley.

Personal planning

People who want to travel on snowy mountains should follow a few simple rules. They should:

- learn about the area—its weather, **snow cover,** and any dangerous areas that should be avoided;
- tell someone where they are going and when they will be back;
- pack the right items—lots of warm clothing, a shovel, a mobile phone or a **transceiver,** and some high-energy food;
- look out for areas where avalanches could happen, including open slopes and valleys and overhanging **snowdrifts** on ridges;
- look out for signs of past avalanches, such as damaged trees;
- travel along valley floors, through dense (crowded) trees and on slopes that are not too steep;
- turn back if there are signs of unsafe snow cover.

Some people carry airbags in their backpacks that inflate if an avalanche hits. These airbags helps keep the wearer near the surface of the snow—a bit like wearing a life preserver in water.

What About Avalanches in the Future?

In the future, as in the past, avalanches will depend on things people have little control over, such as **snow cover** and changes in the weather. However, people can avoid being caught in avalanches by being sensible. If they follow safety rules, build in safe areas, and limit the number of mountain trees they cut down, fewer people will be hurt in future.

Scientists can also help. They are developing better systems to predict avalanches. In Switzerland, electronic monitors around the country measure snow temperature, wind speed, and other things. The monitors automatically send the information to a computer. This computer produces accurate avalanche **forecasts** for each part of the country. Equipment like this will mean that fewer people will be caught in avalanches in the future.

This electronic snow probe is a new tool for measuring the strength of snow layers. It is a much quicker method than digging a snow pit.

Some Avalanche Disasters of the Past

Thousands of big avalanches happen every year. These are some of the biggest and most crushing avalanches that have happened in the past 100 years.

1910, Wellington, Washington
A spring avalanche pushed three trains, several carriages, and a station house over the edge of a cliff and into a canyon 165 feet (50 meters) below.

1915–1918, World War I, European Alps
Avalanches claimed the lives of more than 60,000 soldiers fighting in the Alps. Most avalanches happened naturally, but some may have been triggered by one side shooting into the snow-covered slopes above their enemies.

1950–1951, The Winter of Terror, European Alps
Warm air from the Atlantic Ocean caused unusually high amounts of snow and rain resulting in more than 600 major avalanches. In Austria alone, thousands of acres of forest and several small villages were destroyed. One hundred people were killed.

1962, Ranrahirca, Peru
An ice avalanche near Yungay buried several villages, killing more than 3,000 people. See page 10 for more details.

1970, Val d'Isère, France
A youth hostel was destroyed by an avalanche at breakfast time. Rescuers used plates to help dig out the survivors.

1999, Galteur, Austria
An avalanche that was 1,640 feet (500 meters) wide hit the village of Galteur. Rescuers could not reach the village for 16 hours. They found 23 buried survivors and 31 bodies of victims.

2003, Revelstoke, British Columbia
Two avalanches only two weeks apart—January 20 and February 3—struck a popular ski area near the town of Revelstoke. Each avalanche claimed the lives of seven backcountry skiers and marked the worst year for avalanche deaths in the region.

Glossary

bacteria tiny (microscopic) living things that can cause diseases

blizzard wind-blown snowstorm

climate weather conditions that normally affect a large area over a long period of time

electrocute kill by electric shock

explosive material that blows up, suddenly releasing energy

firewood wood burned to provide heat, often for cooking

first aid first medical help given to injured people

forecast prediction

glacier huge piece of ice formed after snow falls at high altitude

hypothermia when body temperature drops so low that the person becomes sick and could die without first aid

ice avalanche avalanche caused by a large moving lump of ice

institute group or organization of people who work together to learn and teach others about something

pie chart type of graph that divides a circle into slices of different sizes to show different amounts

pollution dirt or chemicals that spoil air, land, or water

power line main electricity cable

ranger someone who looks after a natural area, such as a forest or a national park

satellite object put into space that can send TV signals or take photographs, for example

slab avalanche avalanche caused by the break-up of heavy, solid snow cover or a slab of snow

snow cover snow that has fallen and built up on land

snowdrift where wind has blown snow into a very big pile

snowshoes shoes for walking in deep snow. They have large nets for soles that spread the wearer's weight to prevent him or her from sinking into the snow.

suffocation when someone dies because something, such as snow, prevents them from breathing enough oxygen

terrain shape of land

timber wood used for building

topsoil upper layer of soil

tourism everything to do with vacations, from the people on vacation to the places where they stay and eat

transceiver special machine that makes a signal or message. The signal can be detected using machines called receivers.

trigger set off or start

volunteer person who offers help without being paid

wind avalanche avalanche caused by thick clouds of snow powder in the air

More Books to Read

Drohan, Michele Ingber. *Avalanches*. New York: Rosen, 1999.

Egan, Lorraine Hopping. *Wild Earth: Avalanche!* New York: Scholastic Inc., 2002.

Jennings, Terry. *Landslides and Avalanches*. North Mankato, Minn.: Thameside Press, 1999.

Redmond, Jim and Ronda. *Landslides and Avalanches*. Austin, Tex.: Raintree, 2002.

Yivisaker, Anne. *Avalanches*. Minnetonka, Minn.: Capstone, 2003.

Index